JUSTICE LEAGUE™: OFFICIAL GUIDE
A CENTUM BOOK: 9781911461104
Published in Great Britain by Centum Books Ltd
This edition published 2017
1 3 5 7 9 10 8 6 4 2

Centum Books Ltd, 20 Devon Square, Newton Abbot, Devon, TQ12 2HR, UK
books@centumbooksltd.co.uk

CENTUM BOOKS Limited reg. no. 07641486

A CIP catalogue record for this book is available from the British Library

Printed in Poland

JUSTICE LEAGUE

OFFICIAL GUIDE

centum

MEET THE TEAM

Earth is under attack from a group of alien beings led by a powerful warrior. With Superman gone, and seemingly nothing in their way, who can humanity trust to save our planet from this terrible threat?

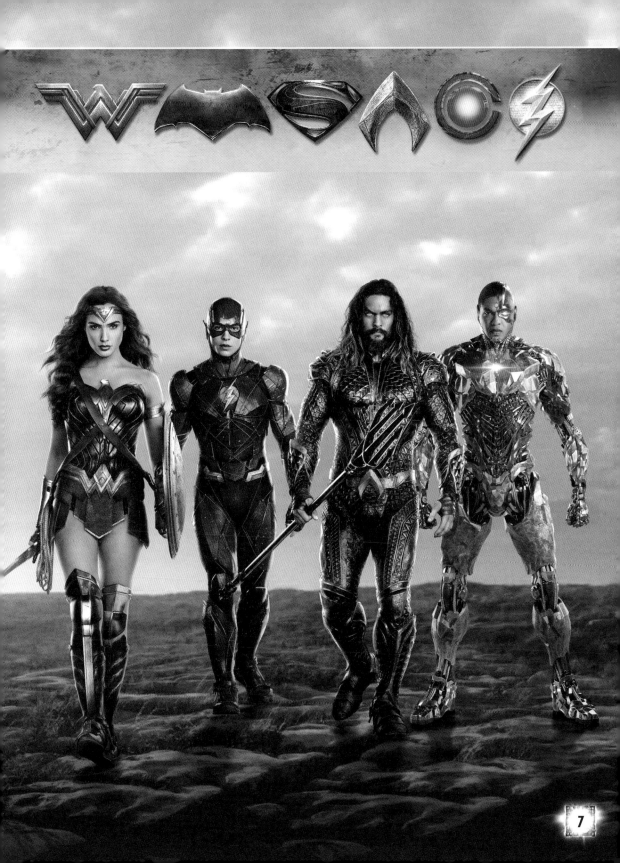

WHAT IS THE JUSTICE LEAGUE?

On their own, even the world's most powerful Super Heroes are no match for the alien invaders. So Bruce Wayne and Diana Prince have joined forces to create a team of super-powered Super Heroes to face this new danger.

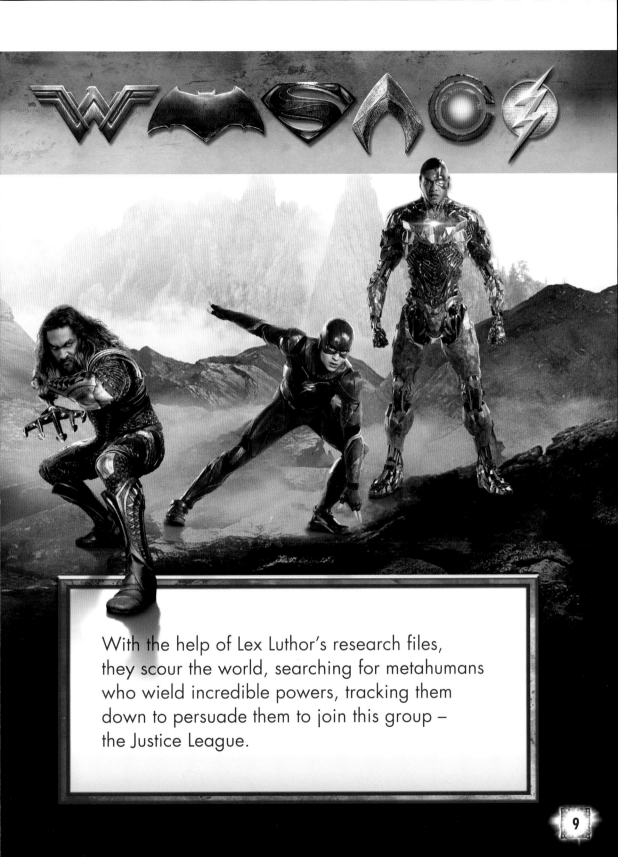

With the help of Lex Luthor's research files, they scour the world, searching for metahumans who wield incredible powers, tracking them down to persuade them to join this group – the Justice League.

MEET THE TEAM

Each member of the team has unique powers and abilities. Though individually powerful, they're not strong enough to defeat these alien invaders alone. They must join forces and work together with one another to create the most powerful fighting force that this planet has ever seen.

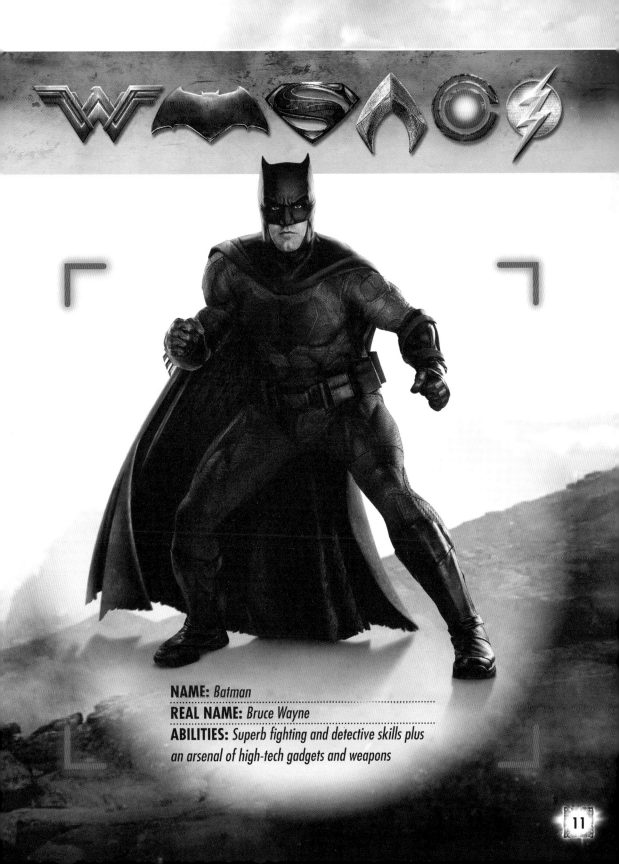

NAME: *Batman*

REAL NAME: *Bruce Wayne*

ABILITIES: *Superb fighting and detective skills plus an arsenal of high-tech gadgets and weapons*

MEET THE TEAM

NAME: *Wonder Woman*
REAL NAME: *Diana Prince*
ABILITIES: *The ultimate warrior who wields a sword, shield, the Lasso of Hestia and powerful gauntlets*

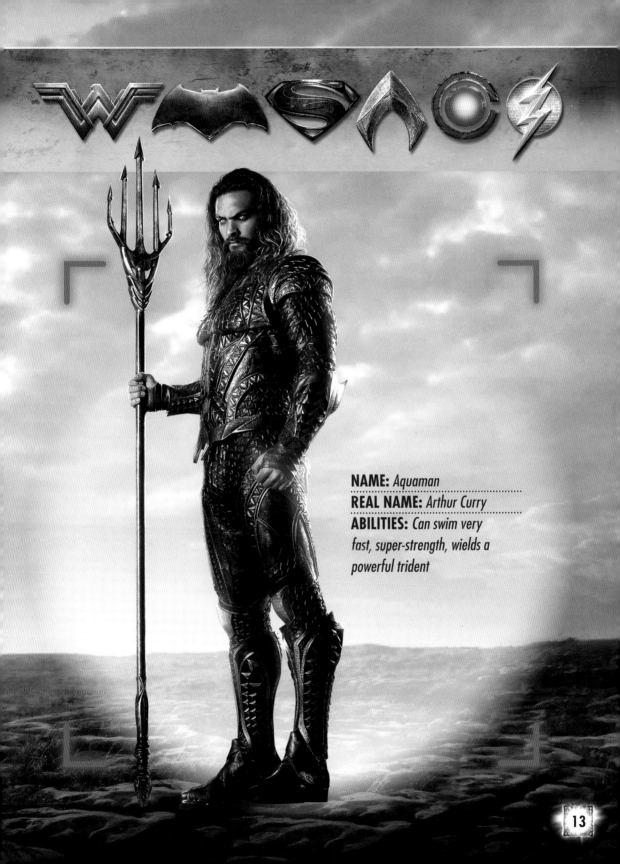

NAME: *Aquaman*
REAL NAME: *Arthur Curry*
ABILITIES: *Can swim very fast, super-strength, wields a powerful trident*

MEET THE TEAM

NAME: *The Flash*
REAL NAME: *Barry Allen*
ABILITIES: *Super-speed and super-healing*

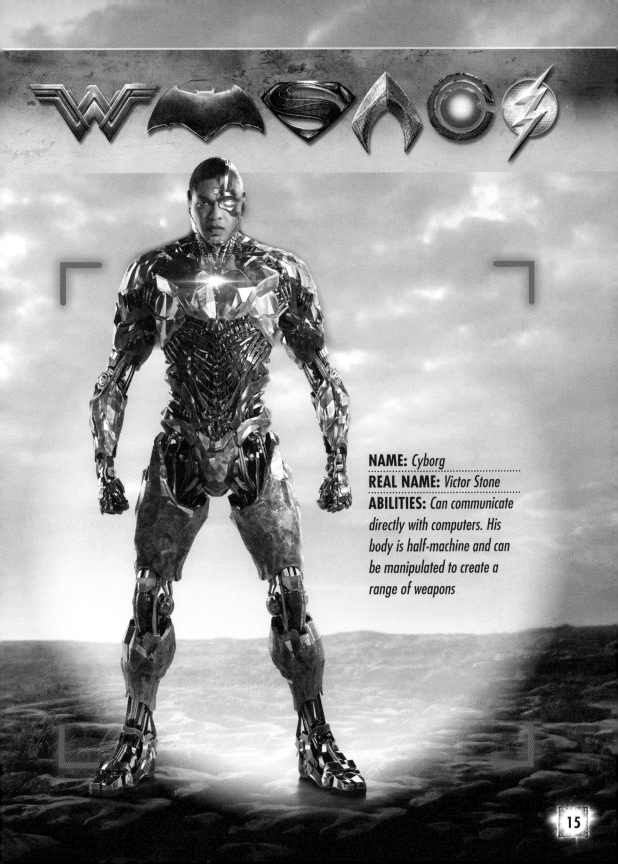

NAME: *Cyborg*

REAL NAME: *Victor Stone*

ABILITIES: *Can communicate directly with computers. His body is half-machine and can be manipulated to create a range of weapons*

MEET THE TEAM

Bruce is inspired by Superman's sacrifice to work with others. His journeys take him to the frozen wastes of the far north to find a mysterious stranger who can swim like a fish. Other potential team members are a little closer to home and can be found on the streets of nearby Metropolis and Central City.

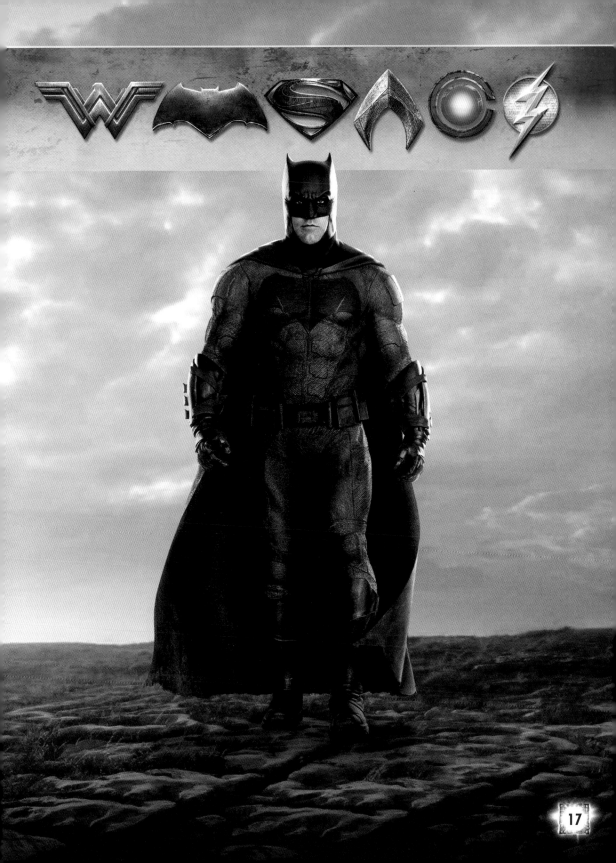

BATMAN

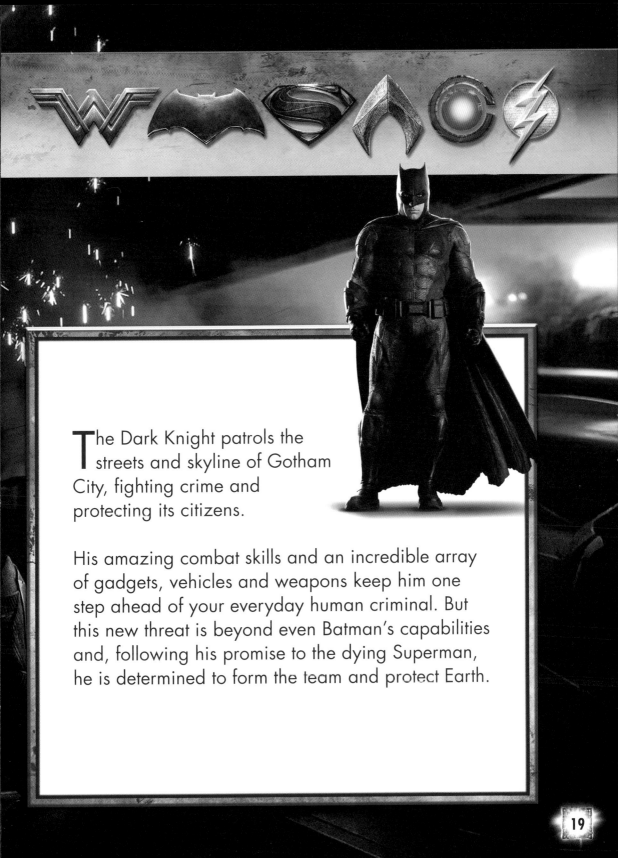

The Dark Knight patrols the streets and skyline of Gotham City, fighting crime and protecting its citizens.

His amazing combat skills and an incredible array of gadgets, vehicles and weapons keep him one step ahead of your everyday human criminal. But this new threat is beyond even Batman's capabilities and, following his promise to the dying Superman, he is determined to form the team and protect Earth.

BRUCE WAYNE

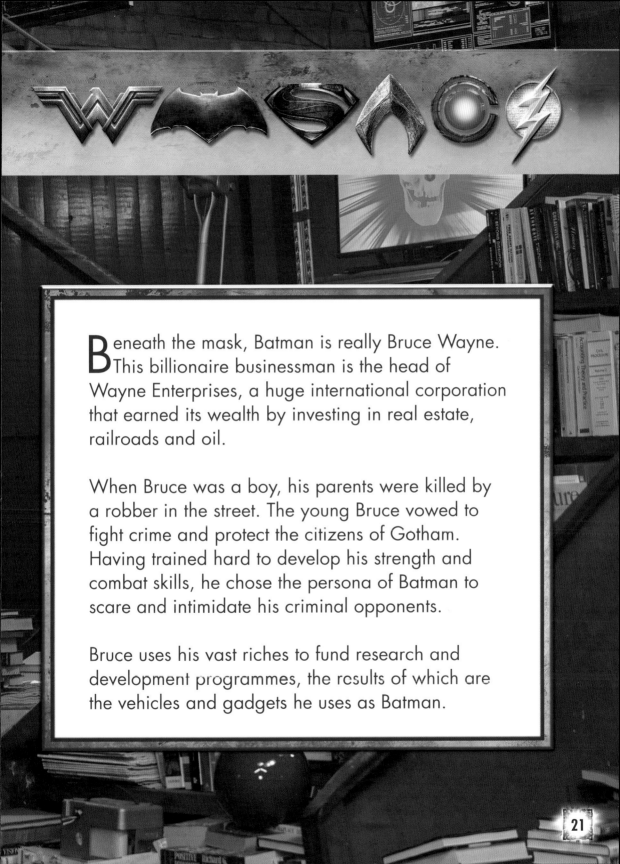

Beneath the mask, Batman is really Bruce Wayne. This billionaire businessman is the head of Wayne Enterprises, a huge international corporation that earned its wealth by investing in real estate, railroads and oil.

When Bruce was a boy, his parents were killed by a robber in the street. The young Bruce vowed to fight crime and protect the citizens of Gotham. Having trained hard to develop his strength and combat skills, he chose the persona of Batman to scare and intimidate his criminal opponents.

Bruce uses his vast riches to fund research and development programmes, the results of which are the vehicles and gadgets he uses as Batman.

THE DARK KNIGHT IN ACTION

Batman relies on stealth, speed and strength to overcome his enemies – and lots of gadgets. He is an expert in unarmed combat, but will use whatever weapons are to hand to fight and defeat an opponent – including his enemy's own weapons!

Using grapnel guns, he can swing from one tall vantage point to another, keeping an eye on the streets of Gotham below. When trouble strikes, he can swoop in undetected and attack the bad guys before they can react.

THE BATSUIT AND WEAPONS

The Batsuit has many roles. It hides Bruce's real identity, allowing him to work in the shadows without being discovered. It also makes him look like a huge bat, striking terror into villains and bad guys. It's also bullet-proof, can protect against knives and has a fireproof cape.

Batman never goes into battle without a small arsenal of gadgets and weapons. Smoke bombs leave the enemies confused, and give Batman a chance to escape, or move into a better position to attack. Batarangs are silent, razor-sharp throwing weapons that can disable a bad guy from a distance.

Grapnel guns let Batman swing from one high vantage point to another in the blink of an eye.

THE BATMOBILE

Part racing car, part armoured vehicle, Batman uses the Batmobile to patrol the streets of Gotham. This rocket-powered automobile is fitted with ultra-strong armour that's tough enough to deflect most bullets and projectiles.

It also runs on bulletproof and flame-resistant tyres. An array of sensors and devices keep Batman informed on the situation and in contact with Alfred back in the Batcave. And, of course, it has an arsenal of powerful Bat weapons . . .

THE KNIGHTCRAWLER

The hybrid electric Knightcrawler was specifically designed to navigate through tight, dark and unpredictable terrain, and is among the most advanced of Batman's vehicle fleet.

With its tank-like abilities, the Knightcrawler can tackle almost any terrain; however, when the tyre treads reach their limit, it's the independently functioning mechanical appendages that allow it to perform such gravity-defying manoeuvers as climbing and scaling vertical walls. In addition, it is equipped with a full arsenal of weapons – from a front tow missile launcher to rear rocket launchers and more – and can be employed by Batman to lead the way into combat.

WAYNE AVIATION

The Wayne Corporation is involved in a lot of businesses, including the development of cutting edge flying machines. Bruce uses this expertise to create vehicles like the Flying Fox.

The largest vehicle in Batman's mobile arsenal, the Flying Fox is a hybrid aircraft with the capability of a bomber and the manoeuverability of a jet fighter. Reaching speeds of nearly 1000 miles per hour with an attack altitude of up to 50,000 feet, it also has vertical take-off and landing abilities.

Bruce Wayne is now finalising updates to the aircraft in the hopes that others will join his fight to defend Earth. As the Flying Fox consists of three large-scale levels and can even transport the newly weaponised Batmobile inside, Bruce sees the troop carrier as the key to conveying the growing League into battle.

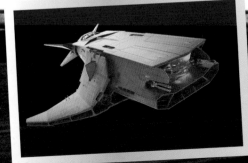

HELPING THE BAT

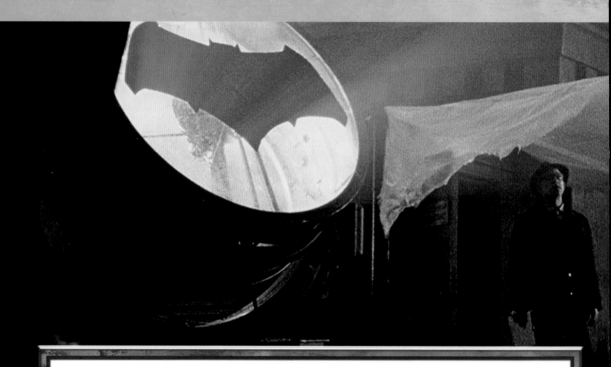

Even Batman can't be everywhere at once, and when Gotham's finest need his help, they use the Bat Signal to summon the Dark Knight. Mounted on the roof of Gotham Police Headquarters, this powerful searchlight throws a dark bat-shaped shadow onto the sky above so Batman knows when his help is needed.

Before long, Commissioner James Gordon will be joined by Batman to find out how he can help.

Alfred Pennyworth acts as Bruce's Head of Security, but he is so much more than that! A former member of the SAS, he is a highly-skilled medic, as well as being an expert at intelligence gathering, driving, and flying. He is also good at fixing Batman's equipment, which is handy as Batman has a habit of damaging everything he uses!

WONDER WOMAN

Princess of the Amazons, Wonder Woman is also a founding member of the Justice League. This immortal warrior has lived most of her life on the mysterious island of Themyscira. A hundred years ago, she travelled to the world of men to help and protect them in times of need. Now, she is helping Bruce Wayne collect together a team of superheroes.

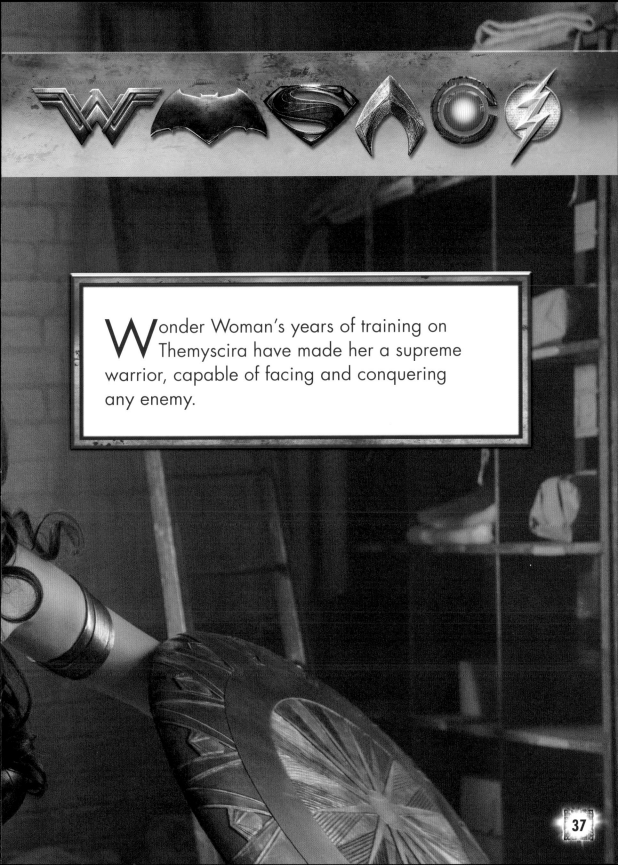

Wonder Woman's years of training on Themyscira have made her a supreme warrior, capable of facing and conquering any enemy.

WONDER WOMAN'S WEAPONS

In battle, Wonder Woman uses a large round shield to defend herself and a powerful Amazonian sword to attack. She wears two bullet-proof gauntlets to deflect projectiles. When these gauntlets are clashed together they produce a powerful concussive blast that can knock down any would-be attacker.

Wonder Woman also has the Lasso of Hestia. Anyone caught in this golden rope is compelled to tell the truth. The Lasso is also incredibly strong, which makes it handy when tying up an enemy.

DIANA PRINCE

Diana has spent a great many years out of the spotlight. But the threat to our planet is forcing her into the open to help Bruce build the Justice League.

42

When she is not fighting as Wonder Woman, Diana Prince is an expert in ancient civilizations and their artefacts. Being immortal gives her inside knowledge into the lives and objects of people who lived a long time ago. This has proved to be very helpful in her job as a curator in a museum.

THEMYSCIRA

The hidden island of Themyscira is home to Diana and the race of Amazons. These warrior women live in paradise, but they train relentlessly for battle so that they are ready to face any danger.

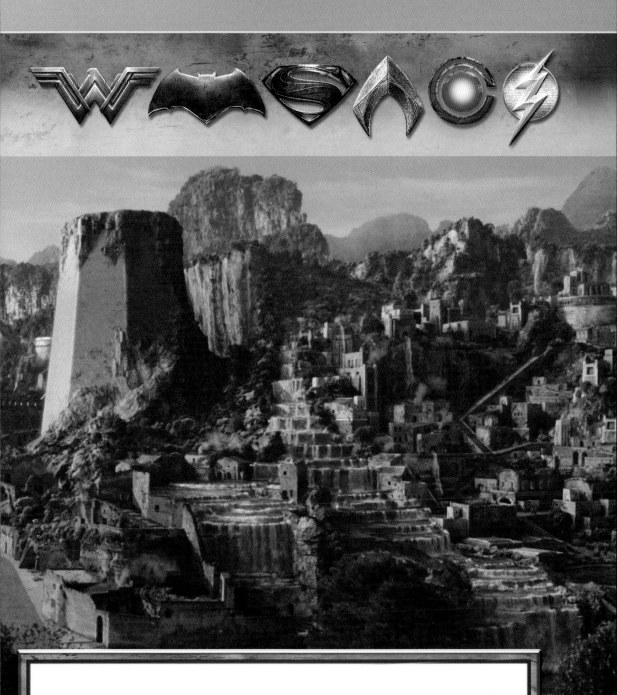

The Amazons also guard a very precious and powerful artefact. When invaders arrive to steal the artefact, the Amazons need to use all of their years of training to face up to this new foe.

THE AMAZONS

Hippolyta is the queen of the Amazons. As their ruler, she has to make sure that they are prepared for any eventuality. Queen Hippolyta has two sisters who are also great Amazonian leaders – General Antiope and Lieutenant Menalippe. The rest of the Amazons are trained warriors who can fight with swords, spears and bows and arrows. They are also expert horse riders.

Stories tell of a mysterious stranger who appears from the depths to help those who have been caught out by the power of the sea. Known as Aquaman, he has super-human strength and carries a powerful, multi-pronged trident.

Although he is powerful, Aquaman is reluctant to take leadership in the world above the waves or in the sea below.

ARTHUR CURRY

Aquaman's real name is Arthur Curry. His father was human, while his mother came from Atlantean royalty. This means that he can survive both above and beneath the waves. His Atlantean heritage gives him his superior strength and swimming abilities, while his human ancestry means he can breathe air that would suffocate a 'typical' Atlantean.

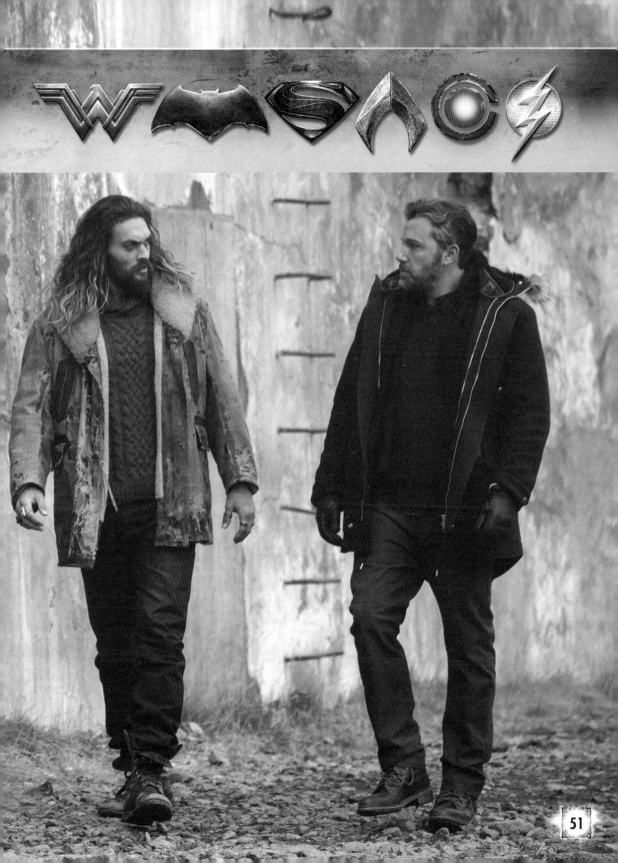

51

SAVING LIVES

This is one lucky fisherman! Aquaman's ability to survive on land and underwater means that he can help sailors in trouble and guide (or carry!) them back to shore.

THE FLASH

With the ability to run at superhuman speeds, The Flash can outpace anything on the planet and dodge bad guys in the blink of an eye.

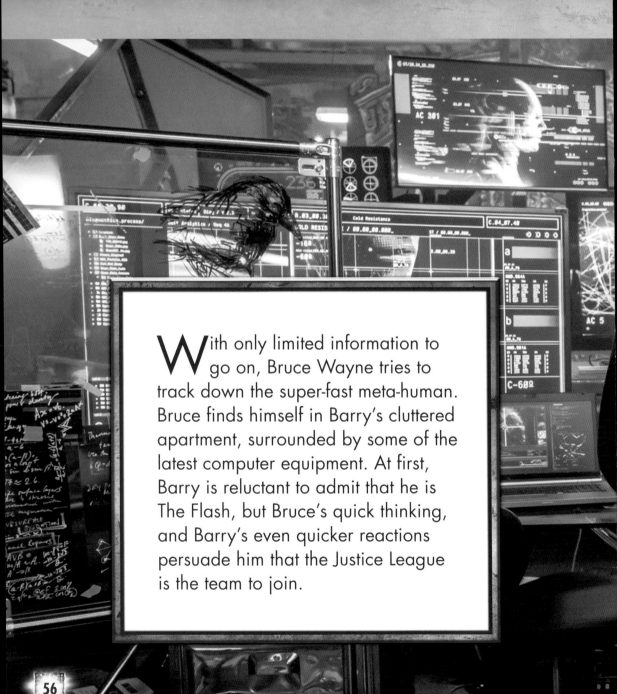

With only limited information to go on, Bruce Wayne tries to track down the super-fast meta-human. Bruce finds himself in Barry's cluttered apartment, surrounded by some of the latest computer equipment. At first, Barry is reluctant to admit that he is The Flash, but Bruce's quick thinking, and Barry's even quicker reactions persuade him that the Justice League is the team to join.

QUICK AS A FLASH

The Flash's super-quick abilities extend to his body's ability to heal itself. After even the most critical injury, his body's cells get to work repairing the damage and, before too long, the wound is healed.

When he is moving at super-human speed, The Flash also generates a huge amount of static electricity. He can unleash this powerful charge in order to blast back enemies or kick-start any piece of electrical equipment.

THE FLASH'S SUIT

The Flash's distinctive red suit has a bright yellow lightning bolt on the chest. It is specially constructed so that it can survive the incredibly high temperatures created by the friction of moving so quickly.

CYBORG

Part-human and part-cybernetic robot, Cyborg is able to manipulate technology. He can communicate directly with computers, controlling them with a simple thought. He can even hack into the heavily encrypted systems of Batman's gadgets and vehicles.

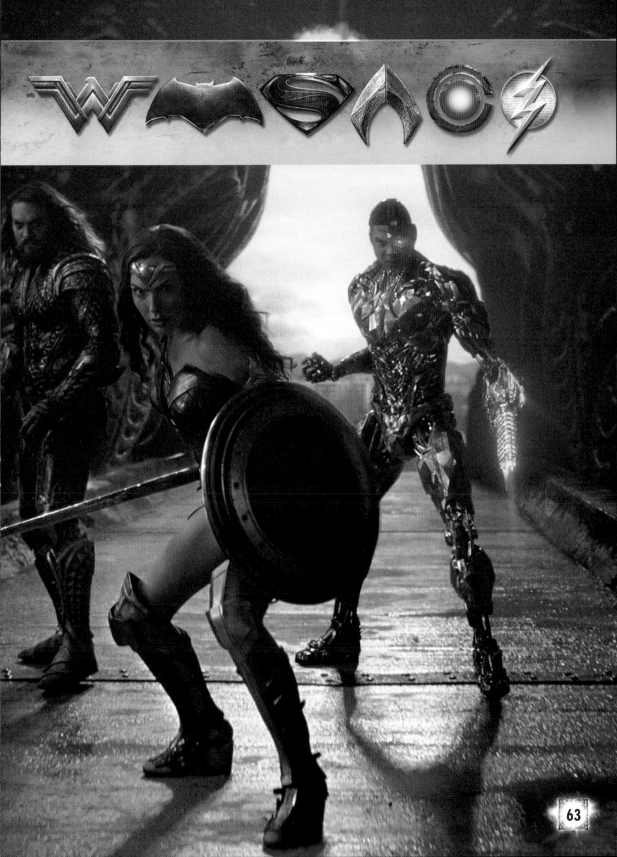

VICTOR STONE

The son of Silas Stone, Victor nearly died in a terrible accident. He was only saved when his father, who works at S.T.A.R. Laboratories, used mysterious alien technology to heal his son. The result was the half-human, half-machine known as Cyborg. Despite saving his life, Stone resents his father and what he has been turned into by the transformation.

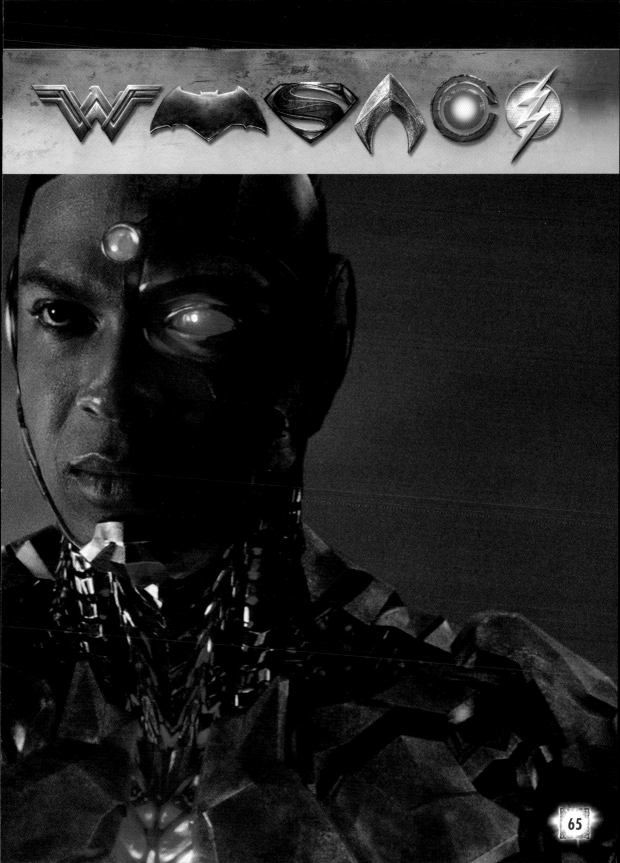

CYBORG'S ABILITIES

Cyborg can fly, has super-human strength and body armour. He also has cybernetically enhanced senses so he can see in infrared and has bionic hearing which allows him to pick up the slightest sounds. Nearly every part of his body has been reinforced with super-tough metal, which means he can survive almost any powerful attack. He can also transform the robotic parts of his body to create powerful blasters.

SUPERMAN'S LEGACY

The Man of Steel made the ultimate sacrifice, dying while protecting Metropolis and Earth from an alien-hybrid invader, Doomsday, that was unleashed by the evil Lex Luthor. Determined to honour his legacy, Bruce Wayne trawls through Lex Luthor's digital files on metahumans in an attempt to form a team of Super Heroes. Only they can protect Earth from the alien invasion Luthor warned Batman about. However, their task would be made a lot easier if Superman was still around . . .

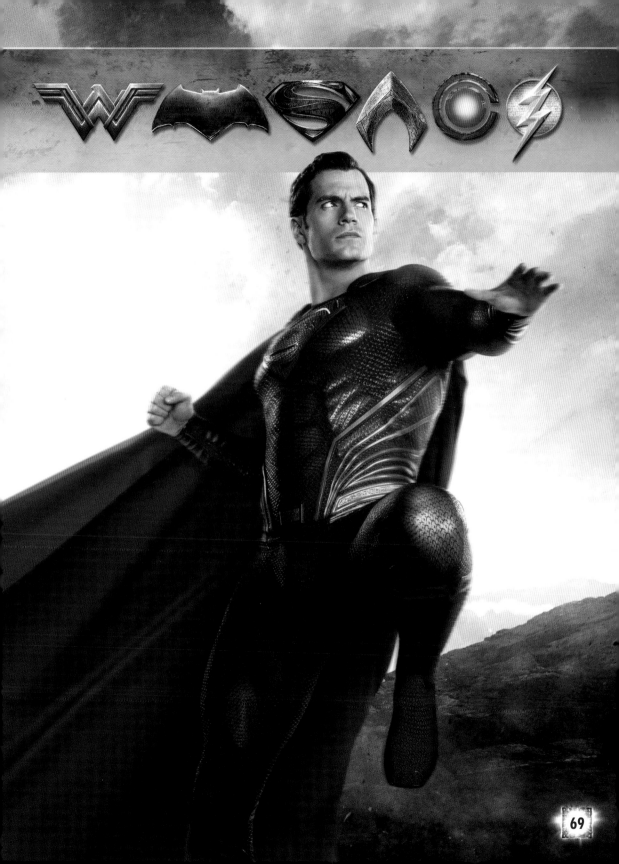

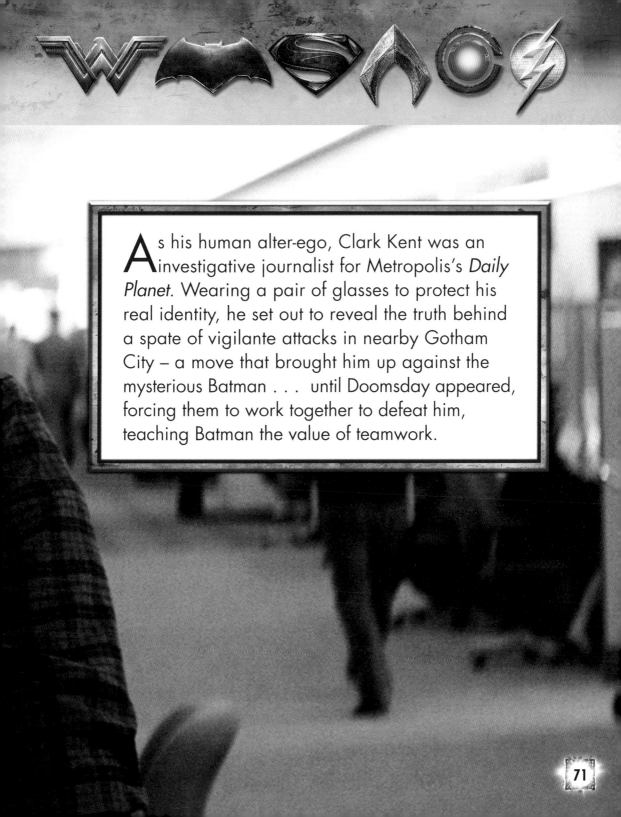

As his human alter-ego, Clark Kent was an investigative journalist for Metropolis's *Daily Planet*. Wearing a pair of glasses to protect his real identity, he set out to reveal the truth behind a spate of vigilante attacks in nearby Gotham City – a move that brought him up against the mysterious Batman . . . until Doomsday appeared, forcing them to work together to defeat him, teaching Batman the value of teamwork.

SUPER POWERS

Having fled his home-world of Krypton just before it was destroyed, Superman was given incredible powers by Earth's Sun. He had unrivalled strength and speed and was able to fly through Earth's atmosphere and out into space. His X-ray vision allowed him to peer through anything, except for lead, and he also had the ability to fire powerful blasts of heat rays from his eyes. All of his senses had been heightened, allowing him to spot things over great distances and detect the faintest sounds. Plus, his super-breath could freeze objects solid, encasing them in ice.

LOIS LANE

As the *Daily Planet*'s best investigative journalist, Lois Lane has reported from war zones and exposed corrupt politicians in her hunt for the truth. She also happens to be Clark Kent's girlfriend. Ever since the death of Superman, Lois Lane has been in mourning for the man she loved. She visits the Superman Memorial regularly to pay her respects to the Super Hero.

S.T.A.R. LABORATORIES

Silas Stone is leading the team of scientists who are investigating the Kryptonian spaceship.

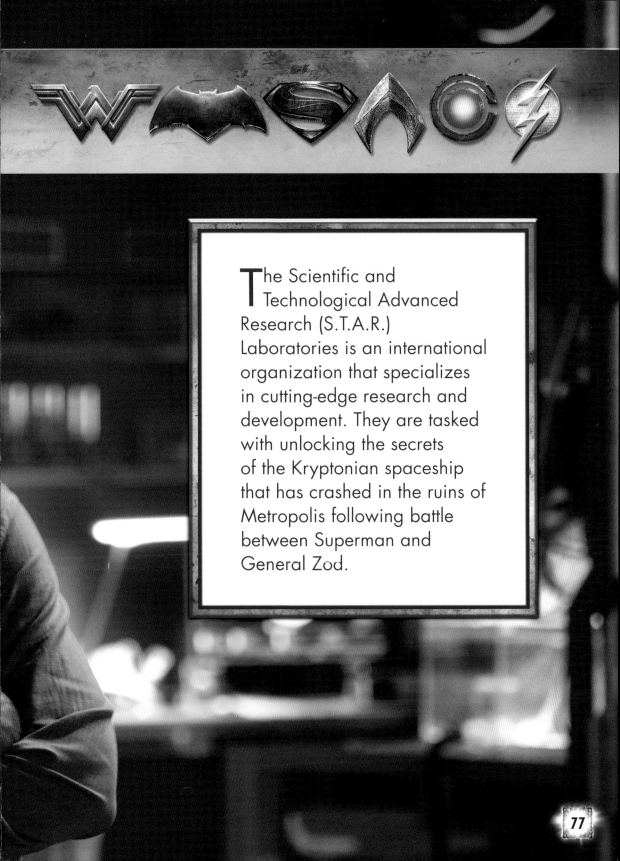

The Scientific and Technological Advanced Research (S.T.A.R.) Laboratories is an international organization that specializes in cutting-edge research and development. They are tasked with unlocking the secrets of the Kryptonian spaceship that has crashed in the ruins of Metropolis following battle between Superman and General Zod.